# The Road to Victory

## A Pre-Easter Home Study

Bill Thomas

CSS Publishing Company, Inc., Lima, Ohio

THE ROAD TO VICTORY

Copyright © 2007 by
CSS Publishing Company, Inc.
Lima, Ohio

All rights reserved. No part of this publication may be reproduced in any manner whatsoever without the prior permission of the publisher, except in the case of brief quotations embodied in critical articles and reviews. Inquiries should be addressed to: Permissions, CSS Publishing Company, Inc., 517 South Main Street, Lima, Ohio 45804.

Some scripture quotations are from the Revised Standard Version of the Bible, copyrighted 1946, 1952 ©, 1971, 1973 by the Division of Christian Education of the National Council of the Churches of Christ in the USA. Used by permission.

**Library of Congress Cataloging-in-Publication Data**

Thomas, Bill, 1965-
 The Road to victory : pre-Easter home study / Bill Thomas.
   p. cm.
 ISBN 0-7880-2440-X (perfect bound : alk. paper)
 1. Jesus Christ—Biography—Public life—Meditations. 2. Bible. N.T. Luke—Meditations. I. Title.

BT340.T46 2007
226.40071'5—dc22

2006032482

For more information about CSS Publishing Company resources, visit our website at www.csspub.com or email us at custserv@csspub.com or call (800) 241-4056.

Cover design by Nikki Nocera
ISBN: 978-0-7880-2440-5
ISBN-10: 0-7880-2440-X                                    PRINTED IN U.S.A.

*To the church family
at Stony Point*

# Acknowledgments

There are some people I'd like to thank for their help in this project.

Thank you ...

- to my parents for all of your support.

- to Claudia Underwood and Kari Lane for all your work on this manuscript and your help getting it ready.

- to Becky Brandt, Missy Cotrell, and the folks at CSS who gave this Easter series life.

- to you, the reader, for your time.

- to the risen Lord Jesus Christ, to him be glory forever.

In memory of a dear friend and member of Stony Point, Mary Szewc. You were faithful in hosting a pre-Easter study in your home for many years. Your love of the Lord and love for people was always evident. I rejoice that you've traveled "The Road to Victory" and have gone home to be with the Lord and with loved ones. Thank you for all you did and all that you were.

# Table Of Contents

**Introduction**   9

**Lesson 1**   11
  Handling Temptation

**Lesson 2**   19
  Noted By Compassion

**Lesson 3**   27
  Being Radical

**Lesson 4**   35
  The Patient Teacher

**Lesson 5**   41
  The Miraculous

**Lesson 6**   47
  A Small Visit Along The Way

**Lesson 7**   53
  The Sacrifice

# Introduction

The title of this study booklet is *The Road To Victory*. The month of March is about "the road to victory." Sports fans will think of "the road to victory" in different ways. Basketball fans know that March is about "March Madness" and the NCAA basketball tournament. Racing fans know that the NASCAR season is very active in March. Baseball fans know that March is the prelude to baseball season. The final days of spring training are important on the "road to victory." Those that follow politics know the significance of March, too. March is the month just before the April primaries. Thus, March is important in the "road to victory."

March is also important in the spiritual sense. Easter comes in between March 22 and April 20. It is calculated each year as the first Sunday after the first full moon after the vernal equinox. That date allows us the opportunity to consider Jesus' "road to victory" throughout March and into April. What did Jesus do in the days leading up to the crucifixion and resurrection? What can we glean from his actions? These questions will be addressed in the next seven lessons.

Each lesson is written so that it can either be taught to a group or used for personal devotion. The lessons can be read directly from the page or the written lesson can be a "springboard" for a leader/teacher. Each lesson contains a scripture reference, a lesson aim, a prayer focus, suggested songs, and thought questions. Feel free to use any or all of them as you wish.

May God bless you this Easter season as you walk "The Road To Victory!"

# Lesson 1

## Handling Temptation

**Scripture Text:** Luke 4:1-13

*Jesus, full of the Holy Spirit, returned from the Jordan and was led by the Spirit in the wilderness, where for forty days he was tempted by the devil. He ate nothing at all during those days, and when they were over, he was famished. The devil said to him, "If you are the Son of God, command this stone to become a loaf of bread." Jesus answered him, "It is written, 'One does not live by bread alone.'" Then the devil led him up and showed him in an instant all the kingdoms of the world. And the devil said to him, "To you I will give their glory and all this authority; for it has been given over to me, and I give it to anyone I please. If you, then, will worship me, it will all be yours." Jesus answered him, "It is written, 'Worship the Lord your God, and serve only him.'" Then the devil took him to Jerusalem, and placed him on the pinnacle of the temple, saying to him, "If you are the Son of God, throw yourself down from here, for it is written, 'He will command his angels concerning you, to protect you,' and 'On their hands they will bear you up, so that you will not dash your foot against a stone.'" Jesus answered him, "It is said, 'Do not put the Lord your God to the test.'" When the devil had finished every test, he departed from him until an opportune time.*

**Lesson Aim:** That each person might come to see that through Jesus Christ he/she can overcome any obstacle or problem.

**Prayer Focus:** Pray that each person might come to see Jesus in a new way and might surrender all to him.

### Lesson

Chuck Swindoll tells the story of "Chippie" the parakeet. It is a good story, so I thought I'd share it with you, too. Chippie never saw it coming. One moment he was peacefully perched in his cage singing, and the next he was sucked in, washed up, and blown over.

His problem started when his owner decided to clean his cage with a vacuum. She stuck the nozzle in to suck up the seeds and feathers in the bottom of the cage. Things were fine, so far. Then, the phone rang. Instinctively, she turned to answer it. She had barely said, "Hello," when there was a "sswwwppp." Chippie had gotten sucked in. She gasped, let the phone drop, and snapped off the vacuum. With her heart in her mouth, she unzipped the bag. There was Chippie — alive, but stunned, and covered with heavy, black dust. She grabbed him and rushed to the bathtub. She turned on the faucet full blast and held Chippie under a torrent of cold water, power-washing him clean. Then, she did what any compassionate pet owner would do: She got the hair dryer and blasted the wet, shivering little bird with hot air. Nowadays, Chippie doesn't sing very much.

Sucked in, washed up, blown over, that sounds a little like us from time to time. Temptation is no stranger to us as we endeavor to live like Jesus. There are times when we are battling temptation that we feel like Chippie. Maybe some of you are in the middle of a crisis. If so, then there is hope. Jesus faced temptation and was an overcomer. You can be, too.

### Background Of The Text

This is the first lesson in a series of lessons that take a look at Jesus. If we are going to get into the Word and get the Word into us, then we need to start by looking at the "Word that became flesh." We've seen Jesus before, but I think we can become too familiar. Let's take another look. Today we see him as "the overcomer." In his story we can see how we, too, can overcome.

This account takes place just after Jesus is baptized. He has come to John in the desert. John is there preaching a baptism of repentance. Jesus comes to be baptized. John doesn't want to do it, but he relents. As Jesus is baptized a voice from heaven proclaims,

"This is my Son, whom I love. With him I am well pleased." Jesus' ministry is starting. He is, at that point, led by the Spirit into the desert. He is there for forty days. The parallels to Israel's forty years in the wilderness are evident. He is fasting and is facing temptations from the devil. At the end of that time, Jesus is hungry. This sets the scene for the next round of temptations.

## The Scene

Notice first, if you are familiar with both the account in Matthew's gospel and this one, that there are a few differences. The order of the temptations isn't the same. Realize that Matthew recorded the temptations wanting to emphasize the "kingdom," so that was listed last. Luke was emphasizing Jerusalem as news of the Messiah spread from Jews to Gentiles. This doesn't invalidate one or the other. The temptations occurred as recorded. The order is not as important as the event.

As the scene opened, Jesus was hungry and the devil came to him. "If you are the Son of God, tell this stone to become bread." The devil was attacking the physical weakness of Jesus. The devil may have been asserting that God provided manna for his people in the wilderness, so surely the Messiah could provide bread for himself. Jesus' response, though, was from Deuteronomy 8:3, "Man does not live on bread alone." Matthew added, "But by every word that comes from the mouth of God." Jesus rebuffed this temptation by noting that his dependence would not be on his ability to take care of his needs. He would rely upon God.

The devil wasn't through, though. Next he took Jesus to a high place, possibly Mount Nebo, and showed him, in an instant, all the kingdoms of the world. It is likely that Jesus and the devil were seeing a vision at this point. "I will give you all of these, with their authority and splendor. It has been given to me and I can give it to whom I want. All will be yours if you bow down and worship me." The thrust of the temptation was clear: "You are the Messiah and you will rule the world. Well, here it is. No suffering." Jesus rejected this temptation, too. Matthew tells us Jesus said, "Worship the Lord your God and serve him only."

The devil had one more attempt. He took Jesus to Jerusalem and had him stand on the highest point of the temple. "If you are the Son of God, then throw yourself down. It is written he will command his angels concerning you to guard you carefully. They will lift you up in their hands so that you don't strike your foot against a stone." This time, even the devil himself was quoting some scripture (Psalm 91:11-12). It isn't quite in context, though. This temptation appealed to the rabbinic assertion that the Messiah would appear at the top of the temple and descend to the people. Jesus' response came from Deuteronomy 6:16, "Don't put the Lord your God to the test."

At this point, the devil left him until a more opportune time. Three temptations and three rejections. All three of these temptations had a basis in fact. All three of them tugged at the heart of Jesus' mission. He refused to submit to any of them. How? Let's take a look.

## The Application
### *The Devil Tempted Jesus*

The first thing we need to recognize is that the devil tempted Jesus. This is significant. Why? If the devil would attempt to persuade Jesus to leave the path of God, then he would also attack Jesus' followers as well. We are open for attack, as well. The purpose of the devil's temptations was to get Jesus to *not* follow the plan of God. He wanted Jesus to sin by deviating from what God had set before him. He is still in that business today. He would like nothing better than for you to forsake God and do your own thing.

How do these temptations come? In all kinds of ways. Some people are tempted to trust in their own ability to provide and make money. "Rely on yourself and do it your way," the devil whispers. "No one will know if you cut out early," he says as he looks around. Others are tempted to find comfort in the "pleasures of this world." "You can't have fun unless you drink," the devil utters. "Getting high is a real trip," he says as he laughs. "No one will know if you watch this movie or visit this website. It isn't really a sin."

All of these are attempts to get you away from the path God has laid before you.

### *The Devil Attacks Areas Of Vulnerability*

The second observation here is that the devil came to Jesus when he was vulnerable. Jesus was hungry. Both Luke and Matthew note that. The devil came at that time, dangling the possibility of food. Jesus is going to be the King of kings. The devil knew about this, too. He offered the kingdoms, pain free, if only Jesus would worship him. The devil was also aware that Jesus was rebuking him with the Word, so he used it, too. *The angels will protect you — God said it.* Jesus, at this point, would have been more than happy to prove the devil wrong and shut him up. He was vulnerable. Realize that the devil comes to us when we are vulnerable, also.

There are areas in our lives where we are weaker than we are in other areas. The devil knows this, too. He attacks when he thinks he can win. He'll attack a marriage when husbands and wives are apart physically and emotionally. He attacks purity when you're alone and it seems as if no one will ever know. He attacks integrity when you're in a position to get by with it. He attacks loyalty when a situation or misunderstanding arises. He sees vulnerability as an opportunity.

### *How Do We Overcome?*

What do we do to be an overcomer? How can we "win" over temptation as Jesus did?

The first suggestion is that we stay busy. Paul writes in 1 Thessalonians 4:11-12, "Make it your ambition to lead a quiet life, to mind your own business, and to work with your hands just as we told you, so that your daily life may win the respect of outsiders and so that you will not be dependent on anybody." The key in this passage is "work with your hands." We need to be busy. Idle time is "risk" time. Notice as an example, King David. When his troops were at war and he wasn't with them, he got into trouble with Bathsheba. Friends, there are all kinds of things that we can and should be doing. Most folks don't have a lot of idle time, but if you do, then use it well. Get involved in helping someone. Be active in your church. There are lots of things for which you can volunteer. Don't let your idle time become an opportune time for the devil.

Secondly, avoid situations of temptation. In the model prayer as found in Matthew 6 Jesus says, "Lead us not into temptation and deliver us from the evil one." We need to make sure that we don't put ourselves in harm's way. This isn't really all that hard. Don't put yourself around the things that tempt you. If you have a tendency to drink too much, then don't start at all. If you can't control yourself on the internet, then don't get on when you're alone. If you have a tendency to gossip, then don't say anything about anybody. If you can't gamble for recreation, then don't go. If your language has a tendency to get inappropriate, then don't ever use certain words.

The final point here is the most important. Jesus battled temptation with the Word of God. All throughout the temptations of the devil, Jesus was immersed in the Word. He used scripture readily. Friends, there is nothing better to battle the lies of the devil than the truth of God's Word. Immerse yourself in the Word. Speak it, read it, know it, and live it. I would advise that not only should we read the Word, but maybe even commit some of it to memory. Fix your minds on what matters and it will not have the time or the inclination to stray.

## Conclusion

Jesus was engaged in battle with the devil at least three years before the cross. Throughout his ministry the devil would attempt to lure Jesus away from God's plan of salvation. Jesus rebuffed all of the devil's attacks. As we prepare to celebrate the resurrection and what that means, the devil will attempt to derail you. Will you endure?

### Thought Questions

1. Jesus was tempted in every way, such as we are, yet without sin. What does that mean for us? What help does that provide?

2. What is the lure of temptation? Is it different for each person? How so?

3. Identify the process in fighting temptation. How can these steps help you remain faithful?

4. What damage is done when we succumb to temptation? What victories are won when we take a stand against them?

### Suggested Songs And Hymns
"There Is Power In The Blood"
"Victory In Jesus"
"Turn Your Eyes Upon Jesus"

# Lesson 2

## Noted By Compassion

**Scripture Text:** Luke 8:40-56

> Now when Jesus returned, the crowd welcomed him, for they were all waiting for him. Just then there came a man named Jairus, a leader of the synagogue. He fell at Jesus' feet and begged him to come to his house, for he had an only daughter, about twelve years old, who was dying. As he went, the crowds pressed in on him. Now there was a woman who had been suffering from hemorrhages for twelve years; and though she had spent all she had on physicians, no one could cure her. She came up behind him and touched the fringe of his clothes, and immediately her hemorrhage stopped. Then Jesus asked, "Who touched me?" When all denied it, Peter said, "Master, the crowds surround you and press in on you." But Jesus said, "Someone touched me; for I noticed that power had gone out from me." When the woman saw that she could not remain hidden, she came trembling; and falling down before him, she declared in the presence of all the people why she had touched him, and how she had been immediately healed. He said to her, "Daughter, your faith has made you well; go in peace." While he was still speaking, someone came from the leader's house to say, "Your daughter is dead; do not trouble the teacher any longer." When Jesus heard this, he replied, "Do not fear. Only believe, and she will be saved." When he came to the house, he did not allow anyone to enter with him, except Peter, John, and James, and the child's father and mother. They were all weeping and wailing for her; but he said, "Do not weep; for she is not dead but sleeping." And they laughed at him, knowing that she was dead. But he took her by the hand and called out, "Child, get up!" Her spirit returned, and she got up at once. Then he directed

*them to give her something to eat. Her parents were astounded; but he ordered them to tell no one what had happened.*

**Lesson Aim:** That each person might see the compassion of Jesus as he prepared for the cross and know that his compassion is available today.

**Prayer Focus:** Pray that each one in your group might come to see the compassion of Jesus Christ and know that he cares for them.

### Lesson

In the 1980s, people shelled out thousands of dollars to own potbellied pigs, an exotic house pet from Vietnam. Their breeders claimed these mini-pigs were quite smart and would only grow to forty pounds. Well, they were half right. The pigs were smart, but they grew to about one hundred and fifty pounds and became quite aggressive. What do people do with unwanted pigs? Fortunately, Dale Riffle came into the picture. Someone had given Riffle one of these pigs and he instantly fell in love with it. The pig, Rufus, was a lot of trouble and never did get "domesticated," but Riffle sold his suburban home and purchased a five-acre farm in West Virginia. Before long, he started taking in other pigs that people didn't want. Now, there are over 180 pigs on the Riffle farm. *U.S. News and World Report* notes that there is a waiting list of pigs hoping to set hoof on the Riffle farm. Dale Riffle explained to the reporter, "We're all put on this earth for some reason. I guess mine is pigs. I'll tell you what is even more incredible than loving these pigs. An infinite, perfectly holy, majestic, awesome God is passionately in love with insignificant, sinful, and sometimes rebellious people. God loves people like you and me."

An incredible story? Yes. A man who loves pigs and a God who loves men. Today we continue our look at Jesus. He is an incredible Savior who demonstrates compassion to those around him.

## Background Of The Text

Today we find ourselves in Luke's gospel, the eighth chapter. Luke is writing to demonstrate that Jesus really is the Christ/Messiah. He wants to provide certainty for the things already taught about Jesus. Jesus, in the eighth chapter, is teaching in towns and villages. He calmed the storm that came up on the Lake of Genessaret. He healed a demon-possessed man. As he leaves the region of the Gerasenes, a crowd gathers. They welcome him. In that crowd, we see a man. He is well dressed and it is obvious that he is respected in the community. He seems to be intent on getting to Jesus. Also in the crowd, we see a woman. She is an older woman. She is standing on the fringe of the throngs of people. She seems to want to see Jesus, but isn't sure. The crowd ignores her.

Two people with great needs and the same hope. Let's see what incredible thing happens.

## *A Tale Of Two Opposites*

The man we met is named Jairus. He is a synagogue ruler and he is desperate to see Jesus. Jairus has a twelve-year-old daughter who is dying. He has tried everything and now Jesus is his only hope. He is the synagogue ruler. For him to come to Jesus meant a great deal. He is acknowledging that this itinerant preacher really is who they say he is. He parts the throngs of people that gather around Jesus. He falls at his feet. He is pleading, "Jesus, come and heal my daughter." Jesus agrees and is on his way to Jairus' house. The crowds are swelling now. Not only have they come to see Jesus, but they will get to see a miracle, too. There is one in the crowd, though, that needs her own miracle. She is hoping to see Jesus, too, but when the man mentions the little girl, well, she knows she can't interrupt that. She thinks, however, if I can just touch his cloak that might do it. You see, she has battled a hemorrhage problem for twelve years. She's been to all the doctors and spent all of her money. She has nothing to show for it all except a stack of excuses and frustration. She is desperate for Jesus, too. She slips in among the crowd as Jesus is walking on the road. She reaches out in a moment of faith and touches the hem of his robe. At once, she is healed. It is a miracle! Incredible!

Jesus stops. "Who touched me?" he asks. The disciples are dumbfounded. Jairus must've been pacing. Peter speaks, "What do you mean, 'Who touched me?' The crowd is huge. It could've been anyone." Jesus insists, though, that someone touched him for he felt power go out of him. At that, the woman comes forward. She knows he knows. "I did," she says meekly. Jesus looks at her with eyes of compassion. "Daughter, your faith has healed you. Go in peace." Incredible!

While they are standing there, an entourage comes. They are from the house of Jairus. "Don't bother the teacher now. It is too late. She's gone." Jesus, though, hearing this statement, looks at Jairus. "Don't be afraid. Just believe." When Jesus arrives at the house, he brings in the girl's father and mother. James, Peter, and John enter, too. A lot of people have gathered. There is much crying. Jesus says, "Don't cry. She's only asleep." They scorn him and laugh. Jesus, though, enters her room. Her body is lifeless on the bed. He takes her by the hand. "My child, get up." Incredible! She sits up. Jesus tells them to feed her and orders her parents not to tell this story.

Two people from opposite ends of society. Both in desperate need of a miracle. In an incredible way, Jesus touches them both. My friends, he is still incredibly compassionate today.

## Jesus' Incredible Compassion Is Seen In ...
### His Time For "Important" And "Regular" Folks

This was a very busy day for Jesus. Two people had great needs. A large crowd had gathered. Jairus, the important leader of the community, needed Jesus badly. An older woman, an anonymous face in the crowd, also desperately desired the Lord. It is amazing that, while on his way to Jairus' house, Jesus stopped for this woman. What does that tell us? Simply this: Jesus has time for all people.

He hears the prayers of presidents and kings. He listens as they describe great and troubling issues. Presidents of our nation, no matter what the political party, have prayed. They pray for wisdom and guidance as they make earth-shattering decisions. Jesus hears those prayers. He also has time to listen to the prayer of the five-year-old child who prays for her puppy because he is sick. It doesn't matter if you've been famous, wealthy, or powerful or if you've just been a "regular" guy, Jesus is concerned about your situation. He loves just the same. He cares just the same. He takes time, just the same. He has time for you.

Some of you here need an incredible touch from the Lord. It is absolutely true that those in Iraq need him. It is also true that those in ravaged parts of our country need him, too. He can handle that, and he can handle what's troubling you. He has time for you and wants to help.

## *His Astounding Power*

By touching his garment in faith, the woman is healed of her hemorrhaging. Power went out from Jesus. That's kind of unusual, isn't it? Power went out from him almost like he was electrically charged. What does that mean? What really healed this woman was her faith in Jesus. She didn't want to bother or keep him from a dying little girl (no doubt, in her mind, a more important case). She simply needed just a touch. That was all. She didn't want to take up too much of Jesus, just a little.

Ellen Corby played Grandma Walton on the former television series, *The Waltons*. You probably know her from that. What you might not know is that she had a bit part in *It's A Wonderful Life*. She plays a customer at the Bailey Building and Loan. George is using his own money to tide the business over during the stock market crash. She is in line to get money. Most are asking for $100. Some $20. She asks for $17.50. That's all she needs. George is touched by her and hugs her.

When I read about this lady with the hemorrhage, I think of Ellen Corby. She only wanted "just enough." She got it! Jesus healed her completely. Compassion came from his heart and lips as he called her "Daughter."

Meanwhile, Jairus is getting nervous. Jesus is coming and that's good. This woman and her problem are slowing him down. I'm sure Jairus is happy for her. I'm sure he doesn't begrudge her healing, but well, come on Jesus. Oh no. It is too late. Or is it? Incredibly, Jesus is not fazed by the announcement of Jairus' daughter's death. His compassion is clear: "Just believe." When they get to the house all the signs of death are present. Jesus ignores them, takes Jairus' daughter by the hand and says, "My child, get up." She does! Incredible.

What does this mean for you? Jesus still has incredible power today and he still cares. The woman who, in humility and faith, just touched his garment, and Jairus, who only had to believe, saw it. You can, too. Will you reach out and touch Jesus? Will you, in faith, believe that Jesus can make what is wrong right again? Just believe.

This doesn't mean that things always work out like we're hoping. His compassion for us is seen in giving us what we need, not what we want. Sometimes the miracle and healing come in a different way. The word to us, though, is still the same. Just believe and the incredible will happen. Sometimes the incredible is healing. Sometimes the incredible is the new job, family, relationship, or situation. Sometimes the incredible comes in the grace to deal with adversity. To you who are in need, Jesus says, "Just believe."

### *The Desire To Come To Him*

A third observation is that people were drawn to Jesus. Crowds thronged around him. People could sense his love and care. Being around Jesus meant something was going to happen. He is still the same today. Jesus would later say, "If I be lifted up, I will draw all men to me." He was referring to his crucifixion and the salvation of humanity. If Jesus is lifted up, presented, people will come.

People today are hungry for the Lord. They want something real; something lasting. Our world today is not a compassionate place. Folks are longing for someone who cares. Maybe some of you are missing something. Maybe you long for the incredible. Has it been too long since you've seen the hand of the Lord at work? Has it been too long since you've felt his compassion in your heart? You can have it again. Jesus the incredible stands before you. He longs to touch your heart and life and make things better.

**Conclusion**

The "road to victory" was marked by the compassion of our Lord. He loves wholly, totally, and greatly. Do you desire his love today?

## Thought Questions

1. What does it tell us about the nature of Jesus that he had time for people of all backgrounds and walks of life? What does that mean today?

2. How do you think Jairus, the synagogue ruler, must have felt as he waited and received news that his daughter had died? What do you think he thought when Jesus said, "Just believe"?

3. Both the woman and Jairus received what they were hoping to receive. How do we respond when the answer is different? Does that change our view of his compassion?

4. How do you answer the oft-asked question, "Does Jesus care?"

## Suggested Songs And Hymns

"Does Jesus Care?"
"I Cast All My Cares Upon You" (chorus)
"No One Ever Cared For Me Like Jesus"

# Lesson 3

## Being Radical

**Scripture Text:** Luke 10:25-37

*Just then a lawyer stood up to test Jesus. "Teacher," he said, "what must I do to inherit eternal life?" He said to him, "What is written in the law? What do you read there?" He answered, "You shall love the Lord your God with all your heart, and with all your soul, and with all your strength, and with all your mind; and your neighbor as yourself." And he said to him, "You have given the right answer; do this, and you will live." But wanting to justify himself, he asked Jesus, "And who is my neighbor?" Jesus replied, "A man who was going down from Jerusalem to Jericho, and fell into the hands of robbers, who stripped him, beat him, and went away, leaving him half dead. Now by chance a priest was going down the road; and when he saw him, he passed by on the other side. So likewise a Levite, when he came to the place and saw him, passed by on the other side. But a Samaritan while traveling came near him; and when he saw him, he was moved with pity. He went to him and bandaged his wounds, having poured oil and wine on them. Then he put him on his own animal, brought him to an inn, and took care of him. The next day he took out two denarii, gave them to the innkeeper, and said, 'Take care of him; and when I come back, I will repay you whatever more you spend.' Which of these three, do you think, was a neighbor to the man who fell into the hands of the robbers?" He said, "The one who showed him mercy." Jesus said to him, "Go and do likewise."*

**Lesson Aim:** That each person might see that Jesus is willing to do what it takes to reach people and so should his followers.

**Prayer Focus:** Pray that each of those in your group might know the touch of Jesus Christ in their lives.

## Lesson

A husband asked his wife, "Tell me, dear, have you ever been in love before?" She thought for a moment and replied, "No, darling. Once I respected a man for his great intelligence. I admired another for his remarkable courage. I was captivated by another for his good looks and charm. But with you, well, how else could you explain it, but love?"

How else could you explain it, but love? I think that describes God's relationship with us, too. Jesus in his life on earth demonstrated some astounding things in the context of love. Today we consider a look at the "radical" nature of our Savior and what impact that has on our own walk with him. Jesus, in this text, offers a glimpse at an "outside the box" life. It is a life that makes a difference. It is a walk that matters. Isn't that what you really want?

## Background Of The Text

The text for today comes from Luke's gospel, the tenth chapter. Earlier in this chapter we find the record of Jesus sending out the 72 to teach and preach. They return with great joy and report that even demons submit to them in Jesus' name. Jesus reminds them that the miraculous is not as important as the eternal kingdom of heaven.

### *The Inquiry*

Jesus then returns to teaching. As he is instructing the people, an expert in the law stands to test him. "Teacher, what must I do to inherit eternal life?" It is the "million dollar" question. Jesus asks him in return, "What does it say in the Law?" He replies, "Love the Lord your God with all of your heart, soul, strength, and mind; and love your neighbor as yourself." Jesus tells him that he has answered well. The man, though, understanding that there is something more asks, "Who then is my neighbor?" Jesus responds with a parable.

### The Parable

A man was going down from Jerusalem to Jericho. This trip was nearly a seventeen-mile walk through rocky and desert country. As he was on the way, he was waylaid, robbed, and beaten. The perpetrator left him half-dead on the road. As he lay there, a priest came by. He saw the man; took a look; but passed. After all, touching him would make him unclean. A second man ambled down that road. He was a Levite, that is, an assistant in the temple. He saw the bloodied man on the road, too. He even went over to get a closer look, but decided it wasn't his place to do anything. A third man came down the road on his donkey. This man happened to be a Samaritan, someone with whom a "self-respecting" Jew would have no contact. He saw the man and had pity on him. He bandaged his wounds and then poured on oil and wine. He put the man on his donkey and took him to an inn; a lodging place for people. He told the innkeeper to look after him and paid him to do so. If he needed any more care, the Samaritan promised to pay it when he comes back.

Jesus concluded the parable by asking the expert in the law a question, "Which of these three do you think was a neighbor to the man who fell into the hands of robbers?" The expert in the law was humbled. We can almost see him gulp as he answered. "The one who had mercy on him." Jesus then concluded the lesson, "Go and do likewise." What an amazing parable! It had an unbelievable ending, if you were a Jew, that is. The Samaritan was the hero. That couldn't be, could it? Jesus has told a radical story to illustrate a radical point.

### What Does It Mean?
*Radical Christians Think Outside The Box*

There are three observations that I think we need to see from this parable. First, "outside the box" Christian faith is demonstrated. In this parable we find three main characters. Three passed by on the road. Two of them were supposed to be men of faith. The priest was a leader in the community. The Levite was a man of good standing. As the story unfolds, the hearers must've thought, "Surely one of those guys will do the right thing." According to Jesus, though, they didn't. They were unwilling to *do* anything to help. They saw the problem. The Levite even went as far as surveying the situation, but when it came right down to it, they did nothing. The one who demonstrated radical Christian faith was the one least likely to do so. The Samaritan traveler. To understand the galling nature of this, realize the hatred that existed between Jews and Samaritans. There was a racial and ethnic prejudice that matched anything of the modern era. As Jesus told this story, his Jewish hearers must've winced as the Samaritan came down the road. Then, notice the actions of the Samaritan. He saw the man. He had pity on him. He bandaged his wounds. He poured on oil and wine. He put the man on his donkey and took him to get care. What made him the hero was not what he believed, but what he did about what he believed.

The same is true today. If you want the "cutting edge," "radical" Christian faith that has substance and meaning, it is seen in what you do. What is "outside the box" Christian faith? Is it going out and living in a cave and memorizing scripture? Well, that's outside the box and maybe even appealing on some level, but I don't think that's what Jesus is referring to here. Is it leaving a job and this country and going to the mission field? Well, again, that's a radical decision and sometimes God is looking for that, but I don't think that's what Jesus had in mind here. Radical Christian faith is seen in the woman who goes every day to the nursing home to visit and care for a friend. Radical Christian faith is seen in the young man who stops weekly to visit the elderly couple and make sure that the grass is mowed. Radical Christian faith is seen in the woman who takes the elderly man to the doctor regularly for checkups. "Wait a minute," you say. "This doesn't sound so radical. These things are the regular, mundane things that people do. What's so radical about that?" That's it. You've got it. Radical Christian faith is becoming the hands and feet of Jesus — doing for others — meeting needs and loving. Jesus said, "If you've done it for the least of these my brothers, you've done it for me."

*Radical Christians Take Risks*

The second observation is that Radical Christian faith is willing to take a risk. The Samaritan was willing to get involved with a messy situation involving a Jew. The priest and Levite saw the situation, but to become involved was too much trouble. The Samaritan was willing to risk it.

Are you willing to take a risk to live the Radical Christian life? Will you risk your reputation among peers to maintain a Christian lifestyle? Will you be radical enough to say, "No, I don't choose to be a part of the crowd — I will do things the way I think God wants me to do them"? Will you be "cutting edge" enough to resist the temptations of the flesh and submit to the Lord? Will you be radical enough to risk your own comfort for the cause of the kingdom? Taking a risk. It isn't easy. Risk-takers sometimes fall. It can be awfully lonely and scary taking a risk for the kingdom. People will question you. They won't understand. They may even criticize. Yes, taking a risk is difficult, but not taking a risk can be devastating. Not taking a risk leads to a life devoid of passion and purpose. Not taking a risk leads to complacency, boredom, and stagnation. The Samaritan took a risk to get involved with the wounded Jew, but the greater risk would've been to walk by.

*Radical Christianity Is Costly*

The third observation is that Radical Christian faith costs something. For the Samaritan, this was true. It cost him financially as he paid for the man's care at the inn. He promised to meet any additional expense on his next trip. It cost him time as he stopped to care for this man. It cost him energy as he bound his wounds and led him to the inn.

If you are going to live a Radical Christian life, it will cost you something, too. Jesus said, "If any man would come after me, he must deny himself, take up his cross and follow me." To live on the edge of faith comes with a price. What is that price, you ask? Jesus wants you to give up your heart, your will, your mind; basically he wants all of you. That's the cost. He wants it all. Now, we've heard this before, right? We even have a hymn that most everyone knows,

"I Surrender All." This isn't a new concept. You're right. It isn't new. It just isn't practiced very often.

Giving all means that your whole life, every part, is under the lordship of Jesus Christ. This means your money. This means your family. This means your entertainment. This means your job. This means your possessions. This means your personal thoughts and habits. This means *everything*! There is nothing in your life that doesn't involve Jesus. You know, I think we've gotten very good at compartmentalizing. We have set up little areas in our hearts, our lives if you will. They are neatly divided and walled off. We get very good at giving Jesus access to most of those rooms. However, for most of us, there is one room that we hang out the "Do Not Disturb" sign. For some, it is the rec room. For some, it is the bedroom. For some it is the study. For others, it is the money room. Whatever it is, we keep that door locked. We say, "Jesus, you can't go in there. That room is mine." Doing that prevents us from living the Radical Christian life that is available to us. Will you, today, throw open the door to the secret room? Will you let Jesus have it all?

### Conclusion

The Radical Christian life is what we all want, isn't it? We want it to be real. We want it to be significant. We want it to make a difference. On the "road to victory" Jesus demonstrated the rewards for a radical faith. Will you live that kind of faith?

## Thought Questions

1. In the parable, why do you suppose the priest and Levite passed the injured man? What does this tell us about them?

2. What do you think prompted the Samaritan to stop? Is this surprising?

3. How would you define the "Radical Christian faith?" Is that something most aspire to live? Why or why not?

4. The author of this lesson asserts that Jesus lived and taught a radical faith. Do you agree with that assertion? Why or why not?

## Suggested Songs And Hymns

"I Surrender All"
"More About Jesus"
"Surrender"

# Lesson 4

## The Patient Teacher

**Scripture Text:** Luke 17:1-10

*Jesus said to his disciples, "Occasions for stumbling are bound to come, but woe to anyone by whom they come! It would be better for you if a millstone were hung around your neck and you were thrown into the sea than for you to cause one of these little ones to stumble. Be on your guard! If another disciple sins, you must rebuke the offender, and if there is repentance, you must be forgiving. And if the same person sins against you seven times a day, and turns back to you seven times and says, 'I repent,' you must forgive." The apostles said to the Lord, "Increase our faith!" The Lord replied, "If you had faith the size of a mustard seed, you could say to this mulberry tree, 'Be uprooted and planted in the sea,' " and it would obey you. "Who among you would say to your slave who has just come in from plowing or tending sheep in the field, 'Come here at once and take your place at the table'? Would you not rather say to him, 'Prepare supper for me, put on your apron and serve me while I eat and drink; later you may eat and drink'? Do you thank the slave for doing what was commanded? So you also, when you have done all that you were ordered to do, say, 'We are worthless slaves; we have done only what we ought to have done!' "*

**Lesson Aim:** That each person might come to know the patience of the Lord and understand his teaching.

**Prayer Focus:** Pray that each in your group grow in their understanding and demonstration of patience. Pray that they also come to recognize what we are to do as followers of him.

**Lesson**

An old legend says that when God created the world, the angels were in awe. As he created the animals, the angels asked if they might have a try at it. God agreed and the animal-creation committee was formed. The committee designed the platypus, a creature with the bill of a duck, the fur of a dog, the tail of a beaver, and the feet of a frog. Since that day, there have been no committees in heaven.

If only that were so on earth, don't you agree? Sometimes we can get tangled in the bureaucracy and red tape of getting through life. We just don't get it, and we end up confused and frustrated. There were times when the disciples felt that way, too. The teachings of Jesus were often hard and puzzling. He demonstrated great patience as he carefully instructed his followers. Today we take a look at some of those hard teachings of the patient teacher.

**Background Of The Text**

The basis for our look into the Word today is a teaching section in Luke's gospel. Jesus has been explaining, in parables, the nature of the kingdom of God. He has addressed the issue of the law and divorce. He told the crowds the parable of the rich man and Lazarus. Now, as chapter 17 opens, he is teaching again. Jesus is speaking to his disciples. We can infer from this that he is addressing a crowd of followers. We also get the sense that as he speaks, he is transferring some important truths, hard truths, regarding living the Christian faith. These teachings seem so difficult that in the middle of this discourse, the apostles cry, "Increase our faith."

What does Jesus say about living the faith? Let's take a look....

**Christian Living Is Evidenced By ...**
*Being Mindful Of Your Example (vv. 1-3)*

Jesus begins by noting the example of every Christian. He says, "Things that cause people to sin are bound to come, but woe to that person through whom they come. It would be better for him to be thrown into the sea with a millstone tied around his neck, than for him to cause one of these little ones to sin. So watch yourselves."

Jesus in this text is warning believers about being mindful of their example. To cause someone to sin, especially one of these "little ones," would bring devastating consequences.

That warning applies to us today, too. We need to be aware of our example and not do anything that would cause someone else to sin. This is a hard teaching but an important one. The call here is to not what is acceptable and right, but to what is best. Our example should be one of the "highest" calling. It is a call to holiness.

We need to ask ourselves this hard question, "Are others led astray by my indulging in 'fun?' " This applies to every area of living. We must understand that people are watching, especially our children.

A little girl of about six was playing in her room with her dolls. Her mother heard shouting and went quickly to her room. She opened the door and saw the little girl pointing at one of her dolls and yelling at her, threatening her. "What are you doing?" the mother asked, somewhat surprised. The little girl replied, "Oh, we're playing house and I'm the mommy and she's the little girl." The mother could only gulp, wondering where she might have learned that.

### *Being Willing To Forgive (vv. 3-5)*

The second teaching of Jesus in this passage is on forgiveness. He says, "If your brother sins, rebuke him, and if he repents, forgive him. If he sins against you seven times in a day and seven times comes back to you and says, 'I repent,' forgive him." Jesus here is noting the importance of being willing to forgive. This is another of those "hard" and "puzzling" teachings. This one is so difficult that the apostles plead, "Increase our faith."

Being willing to forgive is never easy. When we are wronged it is much more "simple" for us to magnify that wrong and dwell upon it. A grudge can build up and soon our outlook is poisoned. Forgiveness, though, can be liberating.

Ask the one who writes to the prisoner who murdered her son.

Ask the wife who forgave her husband's indiscretion.

Ask the parents who reach out to assist the drunk driver who injured their daughter.

I hear what you're saying. "That's impossible. I could never do that." It does sound difficult. To me, though, forgiveness is given when it is first realized. When we accept the forgiveness that God offers, then we are more able to share that same forgiveness.

### Growing In Faith (v. 6)

Jesus heard the apostles' plea for more faith. He replied to them, "If you have faith as small as a grain of mustard seed you can say to this mulberry tree, 'Be uprooted and planted in the sea; and it will obey you.'" Jesus is talking about having a genuine faith that can make a difference. As I hear him say this, I think of his encounter with Jairus. When Jairus was faced with the prospect of his daughter's death, Jesus told him, "Don't be afraid, just believe."

My friends, that is true for us. Faith is knowing that God is going to work all things to the good, regardless of what is seen right now. Faith is trusting that it will come together even when it seems as if all is hopelessly confused.

Have you ever tried to put together a puzzle? Now I know some of you are really into that, but I'm just not all that good at it. My nieces like to do puzzles, but they like to turn them over and mess up the pieces. They expect me to put them together again. Fortunately, they don't do large puzzles. However, I have seen some 1,000- and 5,000-piece puzzles. It seems like they will never get put together correctly. If you just keep working, though, and believing that it will come together, in time it does. I think that's how God works. It seems so big and so disjointed at first. It doesn't seem like it is ever going to be anything. Just keep at it and keep believing. In time, God makes it come together.

### Be Responsible And Humble (vv. 7-10)

The final lesson that Jesus teaches on this day of hard teachings is one of responsibility and humility. He talks of a servant and how the servant is to do what he is supposed to do. His point is clear and comes at the end of the story. "So you also, when you have done everything that you were told to do, should say, 'We are unworthy servants; we have only done our duty.'"

This hard teaching points out the need for humility and responsibility. We are called to do what God has told us to do. He has given each one of us talents and gifts. He expects that we will use them for the kingdom's sake. In addition to the responsibility of doing what we're supposed to do, we are to be humble about it. We are not to brag about what we do or get "big headed" about the things we do. We are not to suppose that what we do is so important or that God couldn't possibly get along without us. We are to recognize that we are servants. We are to do our duty because it is the right thing to do. We do not do what we do for the accolades. We do not expect people to notice. We do not even intend to be thanked for it. We do it because it is what God has called us to do.

## Conclusion

Jesus is a patient teacher. The disciples didn't always get what he taught and neither do we. We are inching ever closer to the crucifixion. Understand what Jesus is saying and what he wants from those who follow him.

**Thought Questions**

1. Are you "mindful of your example"? Identify some of those who are watching you. What do they see?

2. Why is it so "hard" to forgive? What prevents us from really forgiving?

3. Is it hard to trust God when the pieces don't fit? How do we see our faith "increased"?

4. How is humility displayed? Does a humble person know or say that he/she is humble?

**Suggested Songs And Hymns**

"Have Thine Own Way"
"Trust and Obey"
"Humble Thyself In The Sight Of The Lord"

# Lesson 5

## The Miraculous

**Scripture Text:** Luke 4:16-21

*When he came to Nazareth, where he had been brought up, he went to the synagogue on the sabbath day, as was his custom. He stood up to read, and the scroll of the prophet Isaiah was given to him. He unrolled the scroll and found the place where it was written: "The Spirit of the Lord is upon me, because he has anointed me to bring good news to the poor. He has sent me to proclaim release to the captives and recovery of sight to the blind, to let the oppressed go free, to proclaim the year of the Lord's favor." And he rolled up the scroll, gave it back to the attendant, and sat down. The eyes of all in the synagogue were fixed on him. Then he began to say to them, "Today this scripture has been fulfilled in your hearing."*

**Lesson Aim:** That each person might get a new understanding of the miracles of Jesus.

**Prayer Focus:** Pray that each person in your group might know/experience the miraculous touch of the Lord Jesus Christ at this Easter season.

### Lesson

A man, his daughter, and grandson were driving through Pennsylvania Dutch Country. They passed an Amish horse and buggy and the boy's curiosity was stirred. "Why do they use horses instead of cars?" he asked. His mother told him that they didn't believe in cars. After a few moments the boy asked, "Why, can't they see them?"

Sometimes in our lives we fail to see the miraculous. We've been taking a look at Jesus for the past several weeks. Today we take another look at his character, seeing him as Jesus The Miracle Worker.

## Background Of The Text

The text for today comes again from Luke's gospel. Luke is writing a precise account of the life of Jesus to demonstrate the certainty of what has been taught. He has given us several looks into the nature of Jesus. Today we are at the beginning of Jesus' ministry. He is in his hometown of Nazareth. He has been teaching throughout Galilee, but now he is home. He is in the synagogue. His time comes to read the scripture. He then stands to read and from the book of Isaiah he shares these words, "The Spirit of the Lord is on me because he has anointed me to preach the good news to the poor. He has sent me to proclaim freedom for the prisoners and recovery of sight for the blind, to release the oppressed, to proclaim the year of the Lord's favor." Amazingly, he rolls up the scroll and announces, "Today this scripture has been fulfilled in your hearing." Of course, the people in Nazareth reject Jesus as the Messiah. In their minds, he is only a "neighbor boy." That's the rest of the story. Before we move on, though, let's take a look at what Jesus read and how it related to his ministry.

## Miracles Described

The passage from Isaiah 61 describes the actions of the Messiah. He will preach good news to the poor. He will proclaim freedom for the prisoners. He will bring recovery of sight to the blind and release the oppressed. He will proclaim the year of the Lord's favor. These "things" are the signs that will authenticate the Messiah. Jesus is giving these folks in his hometown a preview of what is to come. He will do all of these things. As we read through Luke (and the other gospels) we note that Jesus did miracles.

Who can forget his first miracle, turning water to wine? Remember how he healed the leper with a touch of his hand? Remember his giving sight to the man born blind? Remember how he fed thousands with a few fish and five loaves of bread? Remember his compassion for the widow who had lost her son? He brought the boy back to life. He raised Jairus' daughter. The whole of the gospel account is filled with the miraculous. Let's pause for just a moment and examine miracles. Let's begin by defining a miracle. One of the best definitions I've come across is this. A miracle is the divine imprint upon the world in which we live.

## Miracles Discussed

*Why?*

Let's address some questions regarding miracles. First, we ask why. Why did Jesus do miracles? What was his purpose? A glance through the gospel accounts reveals this to us. Jesus did miracles for a couple of reasons.

First, miraculous signs fulfilled prophecy of what the Messiah would do. The miracles were demonstrations that Jesus was the coming one. The prophets of old told the people that the Messiah would come with the ability to do the miraculous. When Jesus did miracles, these prophecies were fulfilled.

Second, Jesus did miracles to meet the needs of the people he encountered. I am convinced that the miracles of Jesus reveal his compassion for humanity. His first miracle, turning water to wine, was not a public one. It was not done to support any message. It was done because some friends of the family were in trouble and Jesus could help them. Not a glamorous reason, is it? But what an incredible message! Jesus did the miraculous because someone he cared about needed help. What does that tell you? Jesus loves you and cares for you. He can and still does the miraculous. He'll be there for you and provide what you need when you need it, too. As we scan through the miracles, we see a common thread. People are in trouble and Jesus wants to help.

There is a note of caution, though, that must be heeded. Jesus did not heal everyone who was sick. He did not feed all those in the world who were hungry. He did not raise every dead person back to life. His primary purpose was to bring the miracle of salvation to all. Sometimes the miracle occurred in the way desired, but not all the time. Sometimes the miracle is the grace given to endure the problem. Sometimes the miracle is the opportunity to go home to be with the Lord. There are some people that want to equate miracles with a "genie in a bottle." God doesn't work like that. Faith is not measured by how much money you have or by one's health. Faith does not activate God as if he were an impersonal force. Faith is trusting and believing that God does what is best.

*When?*

The next question is when. When did miracles occur? What was the condition present for a miracle to happen? There were some common elements in each miracle account. First, there was a demonstrated human need. Lazarus had died. There was no food. There was a storm on the lake. The servant was sick. The second condition was the element of faith. When interacting with people who desired a touch of Jesus' hand, he always implored them to believe. The belief was always directed at Jesus. He did not want them to "visualize" the person or situation better. He wanted them to believe or trust in him. There were times when Jesus did the miraculous to inspire faith, as well. Faith is connected with the miraculous. The final condition was the presence of Jesus. He was there. He wasn't always visible, but he was present.

What does this mean for us today? I'm convinced that the miraculous still occurs. The conditions can still be present. The problem is that we don't always see the miracle because we are looking for it on our terms. The Lord gives us miracles every day. We just don't pay attention.

Did you notice ...

- the sunrise this morning?
- the beating of your heart?
- the ability to communicate, to love, and to share?
- the changing of the seasons?
- the birth of a child?
- the passing of one from this life to eternal life?

All of these are miracles. We just don't see them because we are not looking.

### *Who?*

The final question regarding miracles is who. Who can receive a miracle? This is the good news. The answer to this question is anyone who trusts in the Lord Jesus Christ. That means that you today can be a recipient of the miraculous. In fact, we already have received more miracles than we are aware of.

Perhaps you are looking for a miracle today. Maybe you are overwhelmed by life's troubles. Maybe worry has bogged you down and you don't think there is any hope. Maybe you need a touch of Jesus' hand. He is there for you. On his "road to victory," he paused to reveal a part of heaven.

### Conclusion

The "Miracle Worker," Jesus, is still in business. On the way to "ultimate victory," let's not forget that, through him, we can win some of the small battles.

### Thought Questions

1. What do you think of the definition of miracle (the divine imprint upon the world in which we live)? Do we see that "imprint" as often as we should?

2. Receiving what we pray for is easy to understand as "miraculous." How is it "miraculous" when the answer is not what we had hoped?

3. Does Jesus still perform miracles in your life? Cite some examples.

4. What miracle listed in the New Testament is your favorite? Why?

### Suggested Songs And Hymns
"Open My Eyes, Lord"
"To God Be The Glory"
"Count Your Blessings"
"Thank You, Lord"

# Lesson 6

## A Small Visit Along The Way

**Scripture Text:** Luke 19:1-10

> He entered Jericho and was passing through it. A man was there named Zacchaeus; he was a chief tax collector and was rich. He was trying to see who Jesus was, but on account of the crowd he could not, because he was short in stature. So he ran ahead and climbed a sycamore tree to see him, because he was going to pass that way. When Jesus came to the place, he looked up and said to him, "Zacchaeus, hurry and come down; for I must stay at your house today." So he hurried down and was happy to welcome him. All who saw it began to grumble and said, "He has gone to be the guest of one who is a sinner." Zacchaeus stood there and said to the Lord, "Look, half of my possessions, Lord, I will give to the poor; and if I have defrauded anyone of anything, I will pay back four times as much." Then Jesus said to him, "Today salvation has come to this house, because he too is a son of Abraham. For the Son of Man came to seek out and to save the lost."

**Lesson Aim:** That each person might know that Jesus cares intimately and has the time and the desire to know him/her.

**Prayer Focus:** Pray that each one in your group might come to see Jesus and know his love and care.

### Lesson

Church signs are helpful and noticed by a lot of folks. Sometimes, though, they can provide a moment of accidental humor. Take, for example, some of these. On a church sign in Florida it said, "The More You Complain, The Longer God Lets You Live." Here's another from Quebec, Canada, "Escape From God, Worship With Us." How about this one from Florida, "11-26-97 Services Canceled. In

Everything Give Thanks." My favorite comes from Kentucky. A singing group called "The Resurrection" was scheduled to sing at the First Baptist Church in Barlow, Kentucky. A snowstorm forced them to have to cancel the engagement. The pastor put the following message on the church sign, "The Resurrection Is Postponed."

Sometimes we just don't quite get it, do we? In the text for today we find a man who, for a long time, missed it. One day, though, Jesus visits and his life is forever changed. It is a familiar story, but perhaps there is more to it than the kids' song. We'll look at the account of the "Wee Little Man": Zacchaeus.

## Background Of The Text

For us, Luke's gospel paints the picture of Jesus as the Messiah, the chosen one of God. Over the last several weeks we have traveled with him on the "road to victory." He is the "one who is to come." Today we find Jesus only days away from his triumphal entry. He is still teaching and proclaiming the kingdom of heaven. In Jericho, however, he has a divine appointment. A short fellow who has been far from God is about to encounter him. Let's look in on the story.

## The Visit Teaches Us ...
### *Things Can Prevent Us From Seeing Jesus*

Zacchaeus was a chief tax collector and a very wealthy man. These are two important facts to notice about this man. Levi/Matthew was a tax collector, but Zacchaeus was one step higher. He was a "chief" collector and, as such, was able to skim even more money for himself. Zacchaeus made a good living collecting what Rome demanded and whatever else he could get to line his own pockets. He was, of course, despised by the populace. For a long time, though, Zacchaeus didn't care. He was content and happy and that's what mattered. One day he heard that Jesus was coming to town. He wanted to see just who this Jesus was. He had heard so much. There was a problem, though. Zacchaeus was too short to see him. It wasn't just his being "height challenged" that prevented him from seeing Jesus. Zacchaeus was also "values challenged." That kept him from the Lord as well.

There are some today in that same boat. What prevents you from seeing Jesus? For some, it is unresolved anger. You've been hurt and frustrated. You're angry. It may not show, but it is there. You're so mad inside that you don't worship. Some of you can't see Jesus because of the hurt you've experienced. Someone hurt you and that just doesn't "go away." You don't think anyone, Jesus or anyone else, can fix it. The hurt that resides in your heart prevents you from seeing Jesus.

Some of you can't see Jesus because of the wall that sin has put up in your life. You'd like to see him, but you can't get over the wall. There are a lot of things that prevent people from seeing Jesus.

## *Jesus Chooses The Unlikely Ones*

Zacchaeus would not be denied in seeing Jesus. He even climbed the sycamore tree to catch a glimpse. Jesus, though, would go a step further. He called Zacchaeus out of the tree and told him that he was going to his house; that he must go there. Zacchaeus gladly came down from the tree and welcomed Jesus. The crowd noticed and began to murmur. "He's gone to be the guest of a sinner." Zacchaeus was the least likely one for Jesus to call out. He was far from pious, but he was the one chosen.

Jesus selects "unlikely ones" today, too. You don't have to have all the answers. You don't have to be perfect. You don't have to come from four generations of Christians. Jesus chooses you. Jesus chooses me.

A little boy came into the pet store day after day. The owner had a new set of puppies and the boy was eager to buy one. After finding out the cost of one, he pledged to work hard and get the money. Every day he came in to visit the dogs and to remind the owner that he was working. The day finally came when the boy had the money. He came into the store with a bright smile on his face. "I've got the money!" he exclaimed. The owner smiled. He, too, had looked forward to this day. "Which do you want, my friend?" he asked the boy. The boy didn't hesitate as he chose his dog. "I want him," he said. The owner furrowed his brow. "Are you sure," he asked, "that one has a bad leg and won't be able to run." The boy only nodded. "He's the one." The owner shrugged and gave the boy the dog he had chosen. The owner watched as boy and dog left the store. When the boy got to the door, he realized why he had chosen as he did. There on the boy's left leg, was an iron brace.

It may not make sense to the world, but Jesus chooses you. He died on the cross to pay for your sin. It doesn't matter what you've done or where you are right now, he wants to come to your house. He chooses you.

## *Meeting Jesus Can Change Things*

For Zacchaeus, meeting Jesus changed everything in his life. He resolved to give half of his possessions to the poor and to repay four times what he had cheated others. It was an amazing transformation. Amazing, but not surprising. Jesus noted that salvation had come to this house. Zacchaeus was not the same person.

You won't be, either. When you allow Jesus to come to you, he changes things. You are not the same. What used to make a difference, doesn't anymore. What used to be important pales into insignificance. You have a new life and a new outlook. This story has been seen in Zacchaeus and countless others. Misers become generous. The crude becomes holy. The broken becomes whole. That's what happens when Jesus comes to visit.

The building was in downtown Kansas City. For a long time, it was an establishment of questionable morals and activities. Let's be honest. It was a massage parlor. About four years ago, the owners of the building weren't able to keep it up and so it was sold. It was sold to (are you ready?) a church. They bought the building and began the process of changing it. Today it is a brand new place. Oh, it is the same building and address, but really, it is new. Why? Jesus is there.

That can be true in your life.

## *Jesus Came To Save The Lost*

That is the most important verse of this entire book. "The Son of Man came to seek and to save what was lost." This was his purpose. This was why he came. He came to redeem the perishing.

He has only a few more steps on this road to victory. He came to find the lost ones and bring them home.

### Conclusion

At the end of the movie version of *Peter Pan*, "the Lost Boys" return home with Wendy and her brothers to find families. It is a wonderful time and a happy ending. The point? Everyone wants a home. That's what Jesus is preparing. That's why he's on the "road to victory." It isn't his victory he's attaining. It's yours.

### Thought Questions

1. The first part of this lesson describes things that prevent you from seeing Jesus. In Zacchaeus' life he was short. His "challenge," though, wasn't just physical. What are the things in your life that prevent you from seeing Jesus?

2. Do you remember being chosen for something? How does it feel to be "wanted"? Do you remember a time when you "weren't chosen." How did that feel? Does Jesus' choosing you have any impact on how you look at things?

3. How would you say "meeting Jesus" has changed your life? Is he still working and changing things?

4. What does it mean to you that Jesus wants to be at home with you? How does it feel that the victory he is winning is yours?

### Suggested Songs And Hymns
"Zacchaeus Was A Wee Little Man"
"I've Been Changed"
"Revive Us Again"
"Stand Up, Stand Up For Jesus"

# Lesson 7

## The Sacrifice

**Scripture Text:** Luke 23:36-46

*The soldiers also mocked him, coming up and offering him sour wine, and saying, "If you are the King of the Jews, save yourself!" There was also an inscription over him, "This is the King of the Jews." One of the criminals who were hanged there kept deriding him and saying, "Are you not the Messiah? Save yourself and us!" But the other rebuked him, saying, "Do you not fear God, since you are under the same sentence of condemnation? And we indeed have been condemned justly, for we are getting what we deserve for our deeds, but this man has done nothing wrong." Then he said, "Jesus, remember me when you come into your kingdom." He replied, "Truly I tell you, today you will be with me in Paradise."*

*It was now about noon, and darkness came over the whole land until three in the afternoon, while the sun's light failed; and the curtain of the temple was torn in two. Then Jesus, crying with a loud voice, said, "Father, into your hands I commend my spirit." Having said this, he breathed his last.*

**Lesson Aim:** That each person in your group might come to a deeper understanding of Jesus' death and what it means.

**Prayer Focus:** Pray that each one in your group begin to comprehend how high, wide, long, and deep is the love of God in Christ Jesus.

### Lesson

Here are some helpful thoughts regarding love and romance. The first question is, "How do people in love behave?" Arnold, a ten-year-old, said, "Mooshy, like puppy dogs, except puppy dogs don't wag their tails so much." Wendy, age eight, added this advice, "When a person gets kissed for the first time, they fall down and don't get up for at least an hour." When asked, "Why do people in love hold hands?" Gavin, eight years old, said, "They want to make sure their rings don't fall off. They paid good money for them." Some final thoughts on love. Jill, age six, said, "Love is foolish, but I still may try it sometime." Dave, eight years old, said, "Love will find you even if you're trying to hide from it. I've been trying to hide from it since I was five, but the girls keep finding me."

Oh the joys of love! Today we consider a familiar text, but one that is tremendously important. It is a story of love; a story of sacrifice. For a few minutes, come with me where we will see love displayed.

### Background Of The Text

We are in the book of Luke once again. Remember that Luke, Paul's traveling companion, wrote this gospel to demonstrate the certainty of the things taught about Jesus. We have been catching different looks at Jesus' nature and character. Today we are at the pivotal point of history. We are just outside the city of Jerusalem. It is a rough, barren place. It is nicknamed the place of the skull. Here we stand before three crosses and watch the condemned die. On the outer crosses are two criminals. They represent wasted lives to this moment. On the center cross, is Jesus. Let's visit Luke's gospel and stand before the cross today.

### What Happened

Jesus has been unfairly tried, convicted, and sentenced to die. He has been led through Jerusalem, carrying the crossbeam. He has been brutally beaten, mocked, and reviled. The soldiers, when they come to the place, crucify him with two other thieves. The words seem innocent enough on paper, but we know the awful truth they represent. Jesus' hands and feet are pierced by a steel spike. He is exposed and bloody. Three crosses jut up against the Jerusalem sky. A swirling mob of hate and anger gathers around the crosses. They laugh at the dying. The one in the middle is the recipient of most of their jeers. Jesus looks into this sea of angry faces and utters a plea. Do you hear what he said? "Father, forgive them. They know not what they do."

Time moves on. The sands in the hourglass fall slowly as death hovers. The soldiers gamble for the clothes of the condemned. The religious leaders are intent on defaming the one called "The King of the Jews." Many of the soldiers, perhaps emboldened by the crowd, torment Jesus. The hate against Jesus is building. A dark shadow is falling, undetected by human eyes. It is the shadow of sin. Jesus is going to bear the brunt of the consequences of sin for all time. The agonizing moment is broken by the strained words of one of the dying. "If you are the Christ, save yourself and us." It is the final, savage mockery from the heart of one calloused and bitter. Before Jesus can reply, another voice cuts through the cacophony of derision, "Don't you fear God, since you are under the same sentence? We are punished justly, for we are getting what our deeds deserve. But this man has done nothing wrong." Finally, words of comfort. They form an island in the sea of torment. Then, perhaps for the first time, the condemned looks to the innocent. His words come forth, "Jesus, remember me when you come into your kingdom." It is a plea of hope. Jesus responds again. "I tell you the truth; today you will be with me in paradise."

Time moves ever so slowly, but it does move. Jesus has been on the cross for almost six hours. A physical darkness has now joined the spiritual darkness. The time of the end has come. The curtain in the temple is torn in two. Jesus cries out with a loud voice. Then these words come from his lips, "Father, into your hands I commit my spirit." Then, he dies.

## What Does It Mean?
### *Forgiveness Is Offered*

Let's examine what Luke tells us Jesus said from the cross. His first words were, "Father, forgive them, they know not what they do." It is an amazing statement of forgiveness. Jesus pleads for those who have mistreated and abused him. He does not seek revenge. He does not ask for them to be punished. He seeks for them to be forgiven.

That is an important message for today. You need to know that Jesus offers you forgiveness, too. For those who think it is too late; for those who think they've strayed too far; for those who think "I'm not worthy"; there is a message of love that echoes from the cross. "Forgive them!" Did you hear those sweet words? "Forgive them!"

Those words mean the prodigal can come home. Those words mean the wayward can get a fresh start. Those words mean the dirty can become clean and the sin-stained soul can be restored. This message is for you, "O sinner, come home."

### *A Second Chance Is Given*

The second words that Luke reports to us come from Jesus to a dying thief. The thief has taken a stand for Jesus. He has rebuked his companion and the angry mob. His only request was wanting to be remembered. Jesus answers him. "I tell you the truth. Today you will be with me in paradise." It is astonishing, really. Jesus acknowledges a man's last dying act and rewards it with paradise. He is the Lord of the second chance, but man, oh, man, what a mulligan.

You see, I like second chances. Some of you have had the rare opportunity to play golf with me. If you have, then you know that I'm, well, just not very good. I do hit about one good shot per eighteen holes. You know what makes me most nervous playing golf? The first hole. You tee off at the tee box and it seems like everyone is watching. I'm secretly praying, "Just hit it in the air about 100 yards. Don't dribble it. Don't dribble it." Invariably, I'll hit the dribbler. How I wish for a mulligan. You see, in golf a second chance to make a shot is called a mulligan. Problem is, you don't get a mulligan on the first tee. I sometimes wish I could get one.

Some of you are looking for a mulligan, too. You'd like another chance at being godly. You want another chance to be a godly husband and father. You're hoping to get a mulligan on being a more Christlike worker. You'd like a mulligan on being a godly mom. You've dribbled your chance, but with pleading eyes you look up and say in hope, "Mulligan?" Here's the good news. You, the criminal and countless others get another shot. Jesus isn't keeping score of "right" versus "wrong." He just wants you to end up on the "right" side.

To your cry of "Mulligan," Jesus responds, "You get another chance."

### *The Way Home Is Cleared*

According to Luke, the last recorded words of Jesus are, "Father, into your hands I commit my spirit." This is also a magnificent statement in what it represents. It means "going home." The obstacles that sin and death posed to keep man from returning to God have been cleared. The road to home is made ready.

Home. The word can evoke many different emotions. It wasn't long ago that Folger's Coffee made quite a use of this imagery in television commercials. Emotional scenes of coming home were played against the backdrop of having coffee. It seems a little strange, but it worked. Why? For a lot of folks the word "home" conjures up warm feelings. It is a time of love, family, and friends. If that's what home evokes in your mind, then Jesus whispers to you, "You can now come home."

For some, though, the word doesn't necessarily conjure pleasant memories. For some, home was, well, not all that good. If that's what you think of, then Jesus whispers to you, "I'll show you what a real home is like."

Whichever is the case for you, home is our final destination. Regardless of the old cliché, you can go home again.

### Conclusion

There is no greater example of love than our story today. Jesus loves you. This is his Valentine to you. It is a card that is heart shaped, but it encircles a cross. The cross is red, the heart is white. The words are simple. They read, "I love you this (arms outstretched) much! Will you be mine?"

**Thought Questions**

1. What does it mean to you that Jesus asked God to forgive those who were abusing him? What does that tell us about him?

2. The author uses the golfing expression "mulligan." Have you ever wanted a "mulligan"? How do you feel that Jesus seems to be offering one to the dying thief? To you?

3. What does the word "home" mean to you? Jesus has provided you with the opportunity to "go home." Is that important?

4. How would you describe the love of Jesus?

**Suggested Songs And Hymns**

"Were You There?"
"My Jesus, I Love Thee"
"Jesus Loves Me"
"I Love You, Lord"

www.ingramcontent.com/pod-product-compliance
Lightning Source LLC
Chambersburg PA
CBHW071759040426
42446CB00012B/2624